Melanchrini

Melanchrini

Maria Taylor

ISBN: 978-0-9570984-5-9

Scan QR code for further title information

First published June 2012 by:

Nine Arches Press
Great Central Studios
92 Lower Hillmorton Rd
Rugby
Warwickshire
CV21 3TF

www.ninearchespress.com

Printed in Britain by:

imprintdigital.net
Seychelles Farm,
Upton Pyne,
Exeter
EX5 5HY
www.imprintdigital.net

Melanchrini

Maria Taylor

Nine
Arches
Press

new poets series

Maria Taylor was born in Worksop in 1978 of Greek Cypriot parents. At the age of six, her family moved to London. After studying at Warwick and Manchester she became a teacher of English and now lectures in Creative Writing at De Montfort University. She also co-ordinates events for the Leicestershire Arts group Crystal Clear Creators. Her poetry and reviews have been published in a variety of publications, such as *The TLS* and in various poetry magazines. She currently lives in the Midlands with her husband and twin daughters. *Melanchrini* is her debut collection of poetry.

For Rosie and Miranda

ACKNOWLEDGEMENTS

Acknowledgments are due to the editors of the following publications in which some of these poems, or earlier versions of them, first appeared: *Cake, The Guardian, Hearing Voices, Ink, Sweat & Tears, Iota, LeftLion, Litter, London Grip, Obsessed With Pipework, Staple, Tears in the Fence, The Coffee House, The Interpreter's House, The Morning Star, The North* and *Under the Radar*.

I am also grateful to the following people for their advice and support: Deborah Tyler-Bennett, David Morley, Roy Marshall, my colleagues Kathleen Bell, Will Buckingham, Simon Perril, and everyone at The Poetry Business. Special thanks go to Jane Commane and Matt Nunn for their invaluable editorial guidance and belief in this collection. I am also indebted to my family who gave me the time to pursue my writing and Jonathan for his unfailing support.

CONTENTS

I

II

III

I

At Her Grandmother's Table

Melanchrini, do you remember the coral morning
when the pigeons gathered in the yard,
soft winged and purling the air with sound?

It was so early when you joined them at the table,
your grandmother spooning out coffee,
placing the mbriki on the stove. Your grandfather sat
hushed and stormless, his eyes filled with wings,
peristeria fluttering. The sun waited a little before rising.

A cockerel crowed daybreak and years went by;
now resting your full-grown elbows on the table
you wonder why it survives to feed you still.

A constant narcoleptic, a dead guest who slept
as in a fairy tale through other people's lives.
Does this table remember the coffee drinkers
who sat by its side singing to a grandchild,
as they reached the grains at the base of their cups?

Melanchrini: dark-featured young woman; *Mbriki*: coffee pot used
for making Greek/Turkish Coffee; *Peristeria*: pigeons

THEA

No one is surprised that her body is mostly broken
or that her bones show through the shrunken outfit
of old age, but there's something of flint about her.
With the others gone she's the only matriarch left.
We arrange chairs around her in a tight semi-circle.

She calls my mother *copella*, meaning lass elsewhere.
An ice-cream van revs through the afternoon's fever
playing a chiming *Lili Marlene* to hot, empty streets.
It's just us, the twenty-first century is having a siesta;
her icons scan me from walls, I keep my knees shut.

Thea would like to know if I'm married, so she asks
my father, who tells her 'yes' and 'to an English man.'
She stares through me to yesterday's village,
where bombs are hidden in melon stalls by heroes
and *levendes*, meaning lads, are hung from ropes.

Asphodel, Revisited

So, after a bit of spaced-out skinny-dipping in the Lethe,
we headed off for a smoke; heads light and stupid,
emerging from the water worse than an unmemoried babe.

I didn't know the names of the others in our ragged formation,
though I reckon the man third from left, sculling and thrusting,
may have been my father. Forgetting's harder than you think.

Lunch is always asphodel petals. We all long for Hades
where there's red meat and wild parties that go on till daybreak.
Afternoons are unceasing here, clouds always bruised.

Idleness is the soil and seed of our souls, but being dead already,
nothing ever grows. I resolve to die again, exhaust the kaleidoscope
of self-harm: pills, blades, hemlock, but nothing. I am still dead.

Now and then I hear them scream in Tartarus. I don't pity them,
skies are red over their way, our fires wheeze ash and black,
dull smoke fills our rusting lungs. As in all things, we stand well back.

A Day at the Races

For over twenty years it's been a cinch,
smiling without any come-on or affection.
Her punters see more of her than their wives,
except nowadays head office calls them 'clients'.

She means business, stacking coppers into towers,
fingers plump but lissome, Claddagh-ringed.
Her name is May, spelt in gold around her neck,
she takes money from an old man, who's busy

watching a screen, purple lips parted, lonely teeth,
as he weighs up the impossible odds, coughing guts
into a damp hanky. *Today's your lucky day* she fibs;
some day she'll drag his sheep-skinned corpse out.

Who dares give horses such indecorous names?
Sam Banjo, Mine's a double, Wholelottarosie.
Cut to ladies, daft complex hats, Lancome smiles,
cut to well-fed gent lifting a ribboned trophy —

'wanker' says the man who's lost all track of time,
making confetti of his hopes on *Walter De La Mare*.
He's itching for a drag of tar but it keeps raining,
fuck it, he snaps, holding his tiny biro like a knife.

SOAPSUD ISLAND

So named because you were London's laundry,
a little islet of suds and labour, importing the dirt
of Kensington and Chelsea, whilst slum-kitten children
mewled around your knees, shedding Mary-blue tears,
and where was mother to clean their faces?

Above a pub, the air sighs with the rags of song and ale.
They bring in the filth through the carriage entrance gate,
see to it all with dolly-peg and mangle, bowls of snow
        and bubble,
restoring the salt-blush to linen cheeks,
sending home virginity like a birthday present.

A hundred years later, buildings lose their relevance,
frigid redbrick covered in mad, mad mouthfuls of dirty kisses,
smut and rain on windows, a church mistaken for a snooker hall,
aerosoled goal posts on its walls, a halation of dreck,
mud-washed halos above the map of your head.

I think of how all your houses have been demolished,
how no one remembers the island.
How I long to scrub and mend, to take an iron
hot from a pagoda stove; straighten and make new.

She is Here

The train's ragged movement suits
her bones, the view is mother's ruin,
a concrete map of haphazard streets;
White City, Westway, Wormwood.

No one saw her pass with a bag
through the ticket barriers, no one
saw her ride the bloodline through
the city. She is seventeen, invisible.

The words she was taught to speak
are strung from asphalt and pitch,
now she'll meet the world head-on,
it will speak a different language.

LARKIN

I

September. Someone hands me a copy of Larkin,
thirty eager teenage faces search me for clues.
I will love teaching Larkin, I will embrace Larkin,
'A' Level Syllabi, York Notes, Spark Notes;
we're going to crack this Larkin like a walnut.

II

October. Larkin has moved in. My photographs
are all of Larkin, the face on the television
belongs to Larkin. In the crisp mornings
birds are tweeting *Larkin! Larkin! Larkin!*
It's Sunday lunchtime, thirty essays on Larkin
scream at me. *Was Larkin a misogynist?*
Was Larkin a misanthrope? Was Larkin a joker?
I give up and go in search of food. Larkin passes me
the leeks and compliments me on my choice of wine.

III

The term ends. We have done our Christmas quiz
on Larkin. 'I hate Larkin,' says a small girl with eczema.

IV

'Tis the season to be Larkin. I go home with a suitcase
full of Larkin. On Boxing Day I drink brandy
and salute Larkin. I think I'm going Larkin.

V

Last night when I was asleep, Larkin was on top
of me again, grunting. His lenses were all steamed-up,
he enjoys the feel of the living, the way we move.
I fended him off with a hardback of *New Women Poets*
and woke up, relieved to see someone else.

VI

You may turn over and begin. Mr. Larkin is your invigilator
for today. I raise my hand, 'How do you spell MCMXIV?'
He clips the back of my ear with a shatterproof ruler.
I draw a Smurf in the margin, I have forgotten everything
there is to know about Larkin. He gives up on me and leaves.
Larkin's shoes echo noisily through the gym.

VII

August. Twisted. They're opening little envelopes,
some smile, some cry. A photographer from the local paper
takes photos of students throwing Larkin in the air.
I'm better now, cured of Larkin. The girl with eczema
has a lighter. I find a charred copy of *High Windows*
behind the gym with a used condom and a can of Lilt.
Never such innocence, as I think someone once said.

AUNTIE

We used to marvel that she hadn't yet died
stunned at the arithmetic of her unceasing life,
the wars, moon landings and assassinations

auntie lived through, as if these events were her,
as if her life were bigger than aphasic bus rides
to supermarkets, laddered tights and polish.

Now Auntie's done, we crush ourselves into
her tiny flat, pretending not to notice anything,
whilst noticing there's nothing to notice.

A cousin by marriage reminds us she was mad;
mad for almost twenty years, this end's a blessing,
his voice sinking into gin, his suit showy.

On her over-vacuumed carpet we leave a trail
of cake and footprint, no cairns or stones,
kicking ourselves for visiting too late.

We search the cupboards just in case, but find
only landfill: we're prying children, falling down
the wormhole of someone else's memory.

After the wake we start bagging and binning.
It's slow work, like clearing a museum
forced to shut, the main exhibit gone.

Mr. Hill

For Patricia

For a while he's gone back to his first wife,
who's decided to keep him on a mantelpiece
with mouth-blown vases on either side.
It means she's had to speak to his mistress.
They have more in common than she realised,
but wonders if her toenails are still painted red.
No one is quite sure where to scatter him,
not her, not their ne'er-do-well grown-up kids,
not even the lady with scarlet toenails.

His wife sits in a sea-fret of white mist,
sighing through her thick cigarette smoke,
she is so confused, she even asks me,
but I'm only a neighbour. For years I thought
he'd already died, the way she spoke of him.
Mrs. Hill takes another drag, decides to post
him back to his lady friend, confiding in me
even though he's dead, he's still a bastard.

EASTFIELD

After the wedding breakfast he put her on a proper train,
with a suitcase full of boutique clothing which went black
by Christmas, though the faux-fur coats survived for bingo.

She told me that keeping clothes clean was a nuisance,
this was coal country, soot ruined the washing,
spread black dust into every nook of their caravan.

She learned to adapt. There was a toothless geriatric
who blew her halitosis kisses every morning, cats yowling
most nights, but that wasn't her reason for staying awake.

She was thinking of the little bird she lost, its limp arms
like featherless wings. My father buried it near the site.
When they choked on their tears, they blamed the soot.

OUTSIDE

When I lift my head and see dusk through a pane of glass
I feel I need to tell you that the petals are still bending to the light
and I need to say that the sky is becoming a painting,
and that each drowsy layer of colour is softening into indigo;
you should also know that birds are still singing over the sound
of cars and bikes; that I love the skyline, its hallowed shapes
and silhouettes, the knowingness of each distant tower.
I stroke your head under my flesh, the moon curve of you.

KIN

When passing through the island
which was your only country,
take in the scent of benign jasmine,
speak softly to travellers on the path,
allow them to speak softly to you.
You won't need a passport or papers,
there will be a glint in your eyes
which is recognised or understood.
They won't be known from photographs
but you will have heard their names
spoken, whispered like incantations.
Eat with them , drink with them,
let them go. When the sun falls
and you must return, lay bellflowers,
take back their stories, and remember
there was no second or third country,
just a place where people came from,
where once before maybe you did too.

APHRODITE AT THE BEACH

Another century spent sunbathing
attracting sighs from love-sick men,
a Greek, an Ottoman, a Venetian
who bowed to her on the beach
wearing flashy, pointed shoes.
She'd grin an alabaster smile
when they wrote her name in sand,
knowing a lacy spew of foam
would wash away their traces.

Now the littoral air is filled
with Russian verbs, other tongues,
and a tired Sri-Lankan emerges
from a shoddy row of beach cafés,
done with grease and taking orders
for a day. Salt brushes his cheek,
he breathes in her scent over brine,
over blue, and feels an urge to sing.

LITTLE ACHERON

You must have sipped from the water
on the night they took you in.
Sometimes I hear the river murmur
when you cry, so I slip underwater.

Hooves suddenly, this is how it feels;
I must have fallen asleep again
so I rise, making sure the curtains
are drawn and notice the cloth is fraying

to a dull peach. Bear with me,
I am not used to the metallic cadences
of machines, or the sight of ghosts
out-staring me in mirrors.

You sleep now, but the river wants
to rush in and I am struggling to keep
the curtains drawn. I breathe in the air
now dense with water, we should be quiet.

Folk Tale

Come here, *copella*, I'll tell you of the old ways,
of how a girl once bore a child, swaddled to sleep
in the threads of a spider's web.

No one chose to marvel his unfathered birth,
no oil, no sign of a cross in dirt to spare him.

The women told her to lie still; she wouldn't fight them.

I Woke into Birth

as if I'd been veined with forgetting juice
as if the room held the whiteness of a moth
as if I were a pin cushion for sterilized sharps
as if a rumpled grin had been sliced into my abdomen
as if surgeons were washing up in the bowl of my womb
as if I were a matryoshka, exposing lathed children
as if the clock's hands pointed like switchblades
as if I were stitched back with threads of spun glass
as if the blood on the swabbed floor were ordained
as if the memory of pain lingered in its withering scent
as if a hunter had slit the belly of a doe to reveal butterflies.

Asleep in an aquarium, I reached for their bodies.

AN UNREMARKABLE WARDROBE

Some thoughts are like wardrobes.
It's impossible to take them anywhere,
so much easier to creep inside, pushing
at the backbone of tigered rosewood,
finding a nook of permanent winter
and a Snow Queen making promises
of sleigh-rides over invisible hills.

And yes, I could leave, but I choose
her glassy world over mine. I breathe
and exhale frail mists of sugared icing,
play among her creatures of stone,
sleeping on bear-skin until I can't recall
the scent of dead women's clothes.
She tempts my lips with cool sweetness,
uneaten platters of Turkish Delight,
teasing *almost, almost but never quite.*

FABLE

The girls pass us by, all volume and lilt
in their weekend tribes, hollering, invulnerable.

We call it a night to the scraping of heels,
sleepwalking through ring-shaped streets

far away from the jewel-box fronts
of shops and bars, into the city's midnight.

We lost the way home under a sickle-shaped moon,
you and I diminishing with every footfall.

I wanted to turn back to the pinwheels of light
thrown from the centre of the city we'd left,

the snaking filaments of liquid electricity
and sticky crowds who shield us from ourselves.

Fable town; our halls of pleasure and distortion,
the absinthe-green light, hollowing your cheeks.

Instead we murmur sobering goodbyes
our voices weaving into the pallium of dark.

You fall into the calyx of my memory
and bury yourself under clocks.

LEAVING

We walk parallel to a city artery,
lupine models snarl on bus adverts,
but no one here has the money.

We walk side by side, but you don't talk,
lost in a world of busy digits,
cursing when your credit expires.

Now you're avoiding the park, its relief,
telling me it's full of murderers, young people
with kitchen knives, mouthfuls of gold teeth.

To me it's a park off the Uxbridge Road
of cherry trees, mandarin twilights: a garden
where oxygen is handed out at the gate.

Thrilled by sepia brilliance, children kick
chestnuts over brittle leaves and listen;
every memory ends in autumn,

a quick chaos of scattering leaves
and wooden fruit that blunt the teeth
falling into unchartered constellations.

Sick of chartreuse and whimsical green,
it was the last autumn for a fire show,
every vein in London was closing.

Sensing impermanence,
I felt the heaviness of falling leaves,
that is to say, their lightness.

99/2000

Our love was still a secret, my mum and dad
thought I was with a friend, not realising that you
were my best one. The hour hand did a final climb
and somewhere around the eight we finished
the last hilarious fuck of the twentieth century
in someone else's living room, the television
gabbled on, reminding us the end was on its way,
reaching midnight, the Queen looking bemused.

I liked the millennium's brief dark. We went out
and crouched on the doorstep, watching fireworks.
We waved at strangers; our skin wasn't our own,
but we were here, we'd made it into January.

Morning floated up, the sky looked down, gave up,
all over Camden Lock everyone forgot themselves,
had the bugs finally arrived, body-snatched us all?
Under the green waves we joked about the trash
and hypodermic needles that must have been there,
a stray, restless cadaver from last night's party.

Joy had congealed, the streets full of refugees,
duvets draped over shoulders, so many escapees
from the past, unable to wander back. Unhistoried,
like the new century, faces young, or maybe young-ish,
with the hangover of all hangovers reeling in their cells.
You said goodbye, the streets suddenly deserted.

I went back to myself, Hawley Road, Castlehaven,
Clarence Way; up my aunt's concrete steps, myopic.
On the mantelpiece, a calendar with an Byzantine icon
of St. Michael, his stiff painted wings trying to open,
my mum and dad wondering how long they'd keep hold,
me saying, 'Happy New Year, I'm here, let's go home.'

BUTCHER

Pausing the cleaver, he tells us how he misses
caper-picking on the hillsides at dawn,
before buds spill their petals, ahead of heat.

Behind me, a row of rabbits are hanging
paw-down from hooks; long and soft-bodied,
each glassy pair of eyes still wet from pain.
No blood on fur, but the smell of it everywhere.

The chopping resumes; he's whistling now,
deftly ordering the chaos of sinew and scrag
into neat piles of hollowed-out muscle,
his board furrowed with trails of blood.

PAR AVION

Air-speeded letters sing the light of home,
lyrical with distance, the blue and red
flecked envelopes become a mother.

Home so far away it turns into myth.
Memory lapses into dream and dreams
are forgotten. The only reality is ink.

Your mother's handwriting, so neat and
clean on the paper's blue, soon spidered
with age; hands tremoring, years passing

like the planes tearing overhead as letters
exchanged over the arc of earth between
a woman and her son, *par avion*.

Faces, half-recalled, revived by pen:
sisters getting married, fathers always busy,
babies getting born, you missing.

Homesickness is an open wound,
you may have thrown the letters away, but
I saw the blood through your shirt.

It spoke with a red mouth.

II

A History of Screaming

In this instance, we'll consider fear,
how it lives in the throat,
how an actress feels its pull,
even before it makes itself heard.

Let me refer to *King Kong,*
you know the film, recollect
the ape's giant bald palm
entering Ms. Darrow's lit room.

Apes, even apes made of fiction,
have instincts; leathery maps
on their palms and soles
instruct their movements.

It's okay. Ms. Darrow was taught
how to scream by her director,
she has learnt how to imitate fear
even with an absence of monsters.

Now it's between her and the ape,
the script has lost its words,
it's all about the perfect little O
of her mouth, a flatlining voice,

shrillness, preternatural fear,
as her bed is pulled and tilted
towards the ape's grasping fist,
as a director's voice echoes,

'You're helpless, Ann, helpless.'

HERE'S TO YOU

We are at the village show,
with diggers dancing, Dexter cattle
and a prize for the longest beans.
The sky threatens rain,
it is at this precise moment
I contemplate infidelity.

He is young enough to be my son,
I notice his smoothness as his t-shirt lifts
his name is Vincent, like the artist.
The V of his pelvis is as they say,
All that. I wonder where the zip
would take me, somewhere starry.

Larry is stuck on a vintage tractor,
inhaling diesel, a woman at a stall tells me
how she has a frozen bat at home
her friend will see to it, a taxidermist
who used to be a midwife; she has
great skill in bringing the dead to life.

I feel a little like that bat,
waiting for a thaw.

ACCORDING TO FOXY

True, you could never keep your mouth shut
so the canal's oily waters would take care of that.
You were warned not to fib, cuss or spill a bean,
as if you could. I imagined your corpse swelling,
a face ribboned with weeds, a sloppy, stupid grin.

Maybe death would come on an afternoon field-trip
where during the final headcount, your absence
wouldn't be noted by Foxy, a ginger-beardy teacher
with a Stalinesque moustache and a rolled-up copy
of *Socialist Worker* peering out from a duffle bag.

He liked badges, strange for a man of his age.
I concentrated on the one that said 'another world
is possible' as he described in an accent, unlike ours,
how canals were not graveyards for the disobedient
but givers of daily bread for the people,

helping a whole generation of Marys and Josephs,
in long dresses and modest cloth caps, to survive,
made real to us from repeats of *How We Used to Live*,
their sturdy horses clip-clopping on the towpath
ropes thrown into sunlight, their children singing.

THREE THINGS I LEARNT IN CHURCH

That I should keep my knees together
That Jesus tasted of fortified wine
That Lazarus pipped him.

EALING HOSPITAL, AUGUST 2000

Frances was in the room diagonally opposite,
her clothes were off again, breasts melted
down her ribcage. She stared at me
as I tried to shut her out with a book.

To my right, the view was vertiginous,
London's skyline made of orange and dusk.
It felt as if my hand could pass through its rectangles
and pale shadow. Sometimes the Eye came into view.

Night fell. Joan talked to her daughters in the dark
around the time of the Coronation, pneumonia
had killed their daddy again. In the morning,
Violet brushed her hair without a comb.
'I'm too young for this,' my eyes said,
Belfast Annie told me to pull myself together.
She wasn't wrong. I got up, taking my drip for a walk.

I put twenty pence in a phone which didn't work,
the currency here was florins and sixpences.
I saw a coffin, seven feet long, floating down the Styx
of the corridor. The ferrymen dressed in uniform.

The night before discharge, defying the rumble of wheels,
I dreamt of sex, the coolness of Long Island Iced Teas.

DELICADO

Martini glass in hand, you gaze into his face
all handsome and candied over with youth,
a quick bite of maraschino from the stick
before he pulls you over to the peach-lit floor,
both of you dancing *Delicado* after midnight,
with your wedding finger newly banded.

It was all orchids then, the world spinning
at 78 revolutions per minute, cherry-sweet,
before your dancing partner found another.
And when I lived in the swaying flat above
your stuck-groove existence, I heard a tremolo
of vibrato notes and glissando scales
drifting up from underneath my heels.
I knew you'd be sinking a melancholy cocktail
toe-tapping *blue star* or *be mine tonight*,
with the band still playing at the Palais Hall
and your glass tremulous and wobbling,
as if it might shatter into tiny pieces.

HALF TERM

Night-shifted, day drifted,
the holidays were over before they began.
My father sleeping on a sofa,
blacked out, like an afternoon eclipse.

I was Pebble-Milled, double-billed,
the world was a snooker ball
sucked into a black hole of a pocket.

When he was awoke for lunch it was
cigarettes, tabloids and betting slips,
two slices of burnt toast, black butter.

A solar flare of anger at a lost race,
then nothing, only the totality of sleep
in preparation for another night-shift.

GULL

I am here, say the voices,
the sky is full of exiles,
scattered so far inland now
you'd think the sea had dried up,
and given away its children.

A long call flusters the air,
voice speaking in stone
a terse, choking language.

One gull lands, squalling at my feet,
spreading a cloak of indignant wings
I throw it a corner of lunch, we meld,
the city isn't happening to us.

They live for thirty years,
                    I remember now,
it could be this very gull that cawed us
from the draize of sleeping Sundays,
untuning what we knew of roof gardens,
parks and playing fields, dreaming them
into beaches and seashores.

Eyes, red-ringed, alert, wings opening
to reveal a temple whiteness of body.

It's always time to leave, to obey flight,
to obey a forward compulsion,
always hungry, moving always.

ESCAPING THE SINGER

My mother worked at the Singer
making women's clothes; stitching,
ripping, changing reels on a spool pin.

Her clothes were going places,
boutiques, parties, after-shows,
draped over bobbing reeds at night

while wearers took a moonlit dip.
When a piece of fuchsia lining
slid from throat plate to floor

I'd pick it up for her, noticing
a river-coolness in the fabric's sheen,
how like water it might seep

from my fingers, headed somewhere.
Though much too young, I knew,
go on, I thought, *take me with you.*

THEODOSIA, LARNACA, 1955

Soldiers at St. Lazarus, sickening for home,
pink as flamingoes crowding the salt-lake in winter,
clustering in huddled stands. Theodosia ponders
overheard church talk, they don't look like devils,
they wilt in khaki, grateful for a friend's cigarette,
tilting their fair heads to the light from a match.

An exchange. She leaves her country for theirs,
Theodosia feels the weight and drub of summer sun
aware that the old life will soon be put to sleep,
yet she is still here, her mother's remaining virgin.
Tea-skinned boys play around uniformed legs
begging for the smallest piece of English chocolate,

shoeless feet making a blur of Cypriot dust.
Theodosia feels a sting as she passes, knowing
dust finds a way into eyes, bringing tears.
She makes her way home to chores in a kitchen,
returning to her mother's side, a living ghost
of blood and bone, they scale and gut in silence.

With the combing of a blade, scales loosen and fly,
knives rip through tangled waves of cord-knots,
heads kept low as hands work at their task
as a sea opens between them, a surge and swell
that carries away children, leaving emptied rooms
and vacant beds, the alpha and omega of loss.

Her mother speaks to virgins at night, but icons
refuse to answer, so the quiet remains by day,
only the little sounds of ratcheting knives
speak for them, as they slit from belly to gill
confronted with the crewel work of the interior,
washing blood from their hands, starting again.

THE YEAR WE DON'T TALK ABOUT

Radio silence. You dial a dreamt-of number
in a phone box, two thousand miles away
at the normal time. Eleni is no longer there,

she lifted your sleeping niece from the cot,
took hold of the little boy's hand and ran,
the keys in her pocket forgot their purpose.

The washing stayed out for thirty years.
Your eldest sister made it back from camp
but wouldn't be big sister anymore.

A receiver fallen from a hook, a siren's tone,
the cratering thud of a parachutist's boot,
the alternative soundtrack for seventy-four.

MY UNCLE'S CREED

I heard my uncle's low-slung notes
before I saw him, a feral litany of bass
pulsing through the grey paving slabs
of Kentish Town. Since he'd given up
on a son and wedlock, it seemed that God
had marked him for a book of psalms.

His eyes scraped across his set face
to look inside the mirror of my own,
but he'd refused to speak, since I married
an *englezo,* so he passed, contriving to groan
Jesus Christ, the saints and the Holy Spirit,
aided by a gargle of communion wine.

He headed towards his wifeless maisonette,
liturgies thrumming with the shoddiness
of all mankind, each vowel pouring like lava
with God slurred in a burning *Kyrie Eleison.*

GETTING RID

To begin, imagine a stubborn bee
in your bedroom. It makes you uneasy,
you want it out, so you tip

a magazine towards its abdomen,
you've been stung before, yet you're fairly
sure you can coax the bee upwards

towards the open window,
you feel the weight of its body
on the pages of your magazine

and there's the vibration of it again,
an angry music in its buzzing
and though you don't speak bee

you know what it means, it fizzes
with determination, this speck of life
thrashing its wings against the air.

SIX WEEKS

last forever, I have compressed eternity
into the red and black squares of a calendar
in my kitchen; an animal prowls in each box.

A high summer afternoon, dense and languid,
English humidity presses down like a thought
on the mind. *Lakes* you think, *Cool breezes*.

THE LANGUAGE OF SLAMMING DOORS

Wind-wracked, each creak and slam
speaks to me; when we moved in
a joiner showed me the clues.

He pointed out the scars;
hinges separating from frames
doors in need of re-hanging.

Right now I'm alone in the house,
listening, as a rush of wind
enters through an open window.

A slam — something of them returns
their children's way of saying enough,
all that's left of echoes of echoes.

III

The Summer of Controlled Experiments

From their awkward position on the field
the skies overhead spell tedium,
an anxious flapping of wings breaks out,
a form of inverse applause.

One of the experimenters vows never again
to wear a dress shaped like a downturned tulip
so unflattering and bulbous at the hip,
without the cover of a cardigan.

Both have noted the dip in temperature
and are discussing supper, no candle lights,
this gnawing need for something bigger.

They walk home in the frowsy rays of dusk,
a palm pressed against a palm
but this is no holy kiss,
they are leading each other to the exit.

ON BEING A MAN ADMIRED BY HEMINGWAY

Sometimes I think of Ernest Hemingway,
full of pipe smoke, talking to a matador
still flushed with victory in the ring
as a bull expires, bleeding into sawdust.

He wants to understand the sensation
of removing a gold brocade before a crowd,
of being a killer, of blood on a spike,
he must be honest in his writing.

On still photographs a bull bleeds
in black and white. Here in Spain
I won't see blood, but I may imitate a man.

I drink with the ghosts of old bull fighters
Belmonte to my left, Romero to my right;
stadiums are empty, no honesty to speak of.

Laying Down a Bone

The phone rang and you already
knew its meaning, so when you hung up
I think you wanted something ordinary to do,
so we played a game of dominoes,
when other things needed your attention.

There was nothing to think about,
we had done this so many times.
Your hands were splayed, faced down
over the black backs of dominoes,
each piece hiding its value and worth.
You mixed the bones for far too long,
with uncertain hands like a magician
whose trick was going wrong,
I think you must have been thinking
about her as you took your time.

MARKET DAY

The man in town who is still angry with the bus driver
who scrutinises every lemon in the market for bruises
who has heard the ground is good to soft at Kempton
who has a surfeit of betting slips in his coat pocket
who ignores the man playing accordion for coppers
who has travelled across Europe with a Weltmesiter
who watches the rainwater pooling in the gutter
who was taught how to play *sevdalinka* by his brother
the music of longing, which repeats and repeats.

THE CARNIVAL OF SOULS

She rises up from the water,
a figurine of dirty clay.

For the spell of the film she's chased,
hell-trilling organs, the undead grinning
at her bedroom window, a letch next door
who offers her coffee in the morning
with company at night. She declines.

The curtains in her room swirl,
like unworn bridal veils. She rejects,
withdraws: men, doctors, churches,
the priest calls it sacrilege. She exits
dressing rooms in silent panic.
The water calls her home again.

She waltzes with the undead
until she expires, beach-snatched
by outstretched, withering hands.
Romero's muse, wooden, frigid,
touched up with Technicolor.

The spell is shoved into film players,
students dissect her with bladed ink,
piercing the flesh of a Cold War starlet
sand-sinking in high heels.

A Little Night Music

After the painting by Dorothea Tanning

She unpeels the brightest petal
with her fingertips

unclothing corolla, the air sweetens

in the music box of her ribs,
busy seedlings rise,

leaves and stems
of undressing sunflowers tendril
in her palms,

she twists the petal handle to free
their tune

her shadow falls, taller than a man,
flower-shaped.

MERMAN

I found him in a fishpond at a lonely end of the park.
His eyes reeled me in, under curdled waves. I felt a hook
pierce at my throat's flesh.

I scooped up his thrashing body, carrying him to my bath.
I sang him underwater lullabies, but his tail stayed fixed.
A fin twitched in place of toes.

Nothing I gave pleased him; roll-mops, fish-sticks, cockles.
Soon, he outgrew my bath, water flowed over the edge
in hot, melancholy sobs.

My tame life was murder for him. He trilled and clicked
in a wild ocean tongue, another world demanded him,
full of reefs, corals, anemones.

He didn't even wave goodbye. I avoided the park, the pond.
I went over to the library, read books about old romantics
who'd lost their mermen, like me.

These women grew old while lovers grew young; taunted
by faces lost to water. Somewhere, we must all be weeping,
in bathrooms, or alone at the bay.

THE CLEANING LADY OF ELSINORE

I could have told them
it was going to end in tears
but nobody was listening.
So, it was down to me again,
to pull on my rubber gloves
and rid the floors of noble blood,
whistling all the afternoon,
not one to grieve, thinking
only makes things worse.

Of course, life's not all soap,
you can't mend what's done.
Elsinore seems quiet now,
survivors keep heads bowed
round disinfected corridors,
as for me, I spit, I polish,
I get on — what's a girl to do?
Elbow grease, foaming water
in a bucket, that would have put
Gertrude's little boy right.

The Murderesses' Cookbook

A kitchen, full of sterile surfaces,
prison spoonfuls of sugar and flour,
telling the younger girls not to fret
if the milk looked like curdling,
Don't worry, she wrote.

Mother Hen, drying her hands
on a tea towel, knowing full well
where they'd been, her method noted
on paper in looping teenage script.

She found new verbs to do the work,
cook, sift, cream, the use of a plastic knife,
If it comes out clean, it's done.

SUPPOSITION

Maybe it began with phone calls,
an exchange of photographs
hurried text messages, then lips,
the bright crimson staining
of beeswax, oil and pigment
over a greedy, wanting mouth.

You walk home through rain
trying not to think the obvious
as water trickles over your face
finding its way onto your tongue
forcing you to swallow deeply,
perhaps it feels like drowning.

In Love

First, dream yourself into a mid-terrace
let flowers grow inside your head.

Rethink the kitchen, see a dining table
tangled with jasmine, petals over tired pine.

Where once you were arm-deep in sink grease,
watch holy roses grow from a plughole

as swallowtails escape from a cutlery drawer
and fly up to a room, not quite your own.

Here are laelia, risen from an unwashed duvet
a mirror all dew, names written in breath.

TOPOGRAPHY

And I think I remember the last time
I saw the terraces, because it may
have been the first. Victorian windows
shaped like tombstones, tenants missing.

I could never place these streets on a map,
I'm not sure they ever existed,
a two-mooned sky in a child's dream.
So many times I have mistaken films for
memories, still the houses fix themselves.

THE PEVERIL OF THE PEAK

Alcopops buried, reborn in spirit, here's
where my friend taught me how to drink
without being a fish. It didn't look much,
a lucky hanger-on in demolition death row,
it did for conversation though.
Smoke clouds
in place of air, waking up with nicotine
weeded in our hair. When we get old we'll say,
'we always had to wash our clothes and hair
the next day,' little smiles on our curly skin,
post-laundered nostalgia, except we'll be saying
it to different people.
Time tumbrills by,
makes wraiths of friends and strangers.

If ghosts exist, the fear is in not seeing them,
not hearing chains clank or seeing a sheeted
figure walk through a wall, wreathed in curling
silver from yesterday's cigarettes.

Perhaps next morning, they'll turn up
pearls of stirred mist in the room's oyster.

Kiss

Nothing hurts quite like the morning,
brittle nails, coffee rings, speeding pulses,
still smarting over another rejection
from the *Interstellar Tantric Poet*.

Your eyes weep from the onion mist
of a night's insomnia, the rising of another
slow dawn over a wall of identical roses.
Daylight forces you down carpeted stairs,
always needing hoovering, never done.

Today you will write a sonnet
about a man who you only know in a poem.
It could be him blowing you a kiss
as you walk through Leicester market,
and this time he isn't being clever or ironic.

Felling a Maiden

i.m. Maria Dimitri-Orthodoxou

And what did she bring to the altar?
A dowry sack of vowels, a grinding toothache
of consonants. In a few inky moments
she would no longer be foreign or hard to spell.

She was not from round here, torn
from fig and oleander, eucalyptus and sea,
though she didn't speak with a faraway voice
or make lace with her grandmother's needle.

After the wedding, I dismembered her.
I placed her in boxes, archived her into files;
her atoms looped among cobwebs and dust,
under attic beams. A suburban oubliette.

I swallowed the heart whole. She was gone.
The silence was everywhere.

Debut
new poets series

Debut is a brand new series of first collections from up-and-coming poets, published by Nine Arches Press. The series represents a selection of the best new voices from the contemporary poetry landscape and work that excites, challenges and provokes its readers.

Since 2008, Nine Arches Press have published over twenty poetry pamphlets and books, including titles which have won the East Midlands Book Award and been chosen as the Poetry Book Society Pamphlet Choice in 2011. As publishers, they are dedicated to the promotion of poetry by both new and established poets, and the development of a loyal readership for poetry. Find out more about Debut and Nine Arches Press by visiting their website at **www.ninearchespress.com** or by scanning this QR Code:

studio harringman

Studio Harringman is a multi-disiplinary creative studio based in East Sussex. For our clients we serve as a complete creative resource; strategy, design and production. We have over 30 years experience in design, branding and advertising. Our client list includes BBC, Thames Television, Universal Pictures, Home Office, Revlon, Warner Brothers, Fremantle and the Shaftesbury Theatre. Run as a family business, the studio was founded by Gary Harringman in 1999 with James Harringman joining the company in 2009. We believe in a world where anyone can publish, quality will always shine through.

www.studioharringman.com